D0783094

The Gruesome Acts of Capitalism

Copyright © David Lester 2006
First printing 2005

Arbeiter Ring Publishing
201E-121 Osborne St., Winnipeg, Manitoba, Canada, R3L 1Y4
www.arbeiterring.com

Printed in Canada
Cover: Mike Carroll
Editor: Jean Smith
Interior book design & illustrations: David Lester
Thank you: Wendy Atkinson, Alan Twigg, Esyllt Jones, John Samson
and Carolynn Smallwood

For other work by David Lester and Jean Smith, visit:
www.myspace.com/meccanormal

With assistance of the Manitoba Arts Council/Conseil des Arts du Manitoba.
We acknowledge the support of the Canada Council for the Arts for our publishing program.

MANITOBA arts COUNCIL
CONSEIL DES DU MANITOBA

Canada Council   Conseil des Arts
for the Arts   du Canada

Library and Archives Canada Cataloguing in Publication
       Lester, David, 1958-

          The gruesome acts of capitalism / compiled by David Lester;
illustrations by
David Lester. — 2nd ed.

(Semaphore series ; 3)
ISBN 1-894037-30-8
978-1894037-30-3

       1. Income distribution--Statistics. 2. Poverty--Statistics. 3. Capitalism--Social aspects.
4. Globalization--Social aspects. I. Lester, David, 1958- II. Series.
JZ1318.G78 2006   339.202'1   C2006-906325-7

THE GRUESOME ACTS
OF CAPITALISM

DAVID LESTER

ARBEITER RING PUBLISHING • WINNIPEG

"I keep on underestimating capitalism. I regard it as the world's evil, and I still continue to underestimate it..."

— **Stephen Lewis**, United Nations Special Envoy
for HIV/AIDS in Africa, 2006

"I've made a lot of decisions along the way for the whole purpose of not being involved in the corporate culture, of not participating in perpetuating what I see as a complete takeover—not only of culture and of media but of government, of politics. I mean, you have corporate advertisements in schools now for the youngest of age groups, and commercially operated TV being shown in classrooms as an 'educational tool.'"

— **Ani Difranco**, musician and business owner, 2001

"A true revolution of values will soon look uneasily on the glaring contrast of poverty and wealth. With righteous indignation, it will look across the seas and see individual capitalists of the West investing huge sums of money in Asia, Africa, and South America, only to take the profits out with no concern for the social betterment of the countries, and say, 'This is not just.' It will look at our alliance with the landed gentry of South America and say, 'This is not just.' The Western arrogance of feeling that it has everything to teach others and nothing to learn from them is not just."

— **Martin Luther King**, civil rights leader, 1967

"So we get people who just see profit as important. Money, money and more money. That doesn't go together with inner spiritual development."

— **Dalai Lama**, Tibetan spiritual leader, 2006

CONTENTS

The chapters have been divided by the names of historical figures whose struggles against inequalities are fitting reminders of what is possible.

Money is in U.S. funds unless otherwise stated.

Preface
by JEAN SMITH

Jack contacted our band, Mecca Normal, several years ago and offered to create our first website. After that he took digital photos of our artwork and then he gave me two computers. Jack has continued to help us, and somewhere along the way, we became friends. Jack values the live music scene he participates in as an audience member. He goes to shows and thinks about what musicians endure to make things happen — he doesn't just pay the cover, buy a CD and go home. In deciding to be useful to the process, he created his own role in underground culture. His contribution has made his experience more interesting and his support has pulled us through some dark times. Reciprocity is an important component of underground and D-I-Y culture scenes.

An example of consumer/artist disconnect is on the Mecca Normal merch table at our shows — the chapbook edition of *Gruesome Acts of Capitalism*. People pick it up, read it cover to cover, put it down and walk away. Consumers expect to be exposed to products and stimuli without considering their value from perspectives other than desirability and cost.

"Who cares if there's underground culture or not? Gap-Coke-Sony-Time-Warner satisfies our needs... don't they?" David Lester and I answer this question in our lecture "How Art and Music Can Change The World" which we put together to expand beyond night clubs and bars, to reveal the behind-the-scenes art and music partnership we have maintained for over twenty years. Our lecture intends to inspire students to include political ideas in their self-expression and to recognize that the life of an artist is not entirely glamorous.

———————

At 6:45 a.m. I'm striding past Starbucks on my way to work at Curves, the gym for women. I decide to get a muffin at McDonald's rather than the independently owned Laughing Bean where the muffins are better, but twice the price. The woman serving me at McDonald's laughs when I ask her for the biggest muffin. She says, "They're all the same size." As she wraps it up I say, "One may as well ask for what one wants in life, even if it is only for the biggest muffin." At the gym I tell two members, "I have done something bad. I bought a muffin at McDonald's." One of the members says, "Doing the best you can most of the time is basically good enough."

My co-worker, twenty-year-old Lindy tells me she wants to open a multiplex school for theatre, music and gymnastics. I say, "That sounds like such an exciting plan!" Lindy frowns, slumps down into the swivel chair and says, "Jean, are you making fun of me?" I say, "No Lindy! You have a good heart and you have so much to share. I think it's a great idea!" Lindy sips her cappuccino and says, "I don't see how I'll ever get the money together. The bus costs $4.50 a day, I work part-time at $9 an hour and I just spent $7 on this coffee and a sandwich." I do the math — Lindy's expenses total over 30% of her gross pay.

Rueben lives in a big house on island acreage. In his youth he was a communist, but now, in his late fifties, he is hell-bent on protecting his privileges. Rueben is concerned that this book makes an inaccurate connection between the amount of perfume bought in France and poverty in Africa; he believes that the average lumpen reader will assume that wealth in the west causes poverty elsewhere. Rueben would be a happier man if the USA occupied and maintained forces in every country in the world. Rueben believes that if an artist cannot earn a living with their art they need to stop making art and get a job.

To paraphrase Greenpeace historian Rex Weyler, when you see your culture is going in the wrong direction, you have to stop, get out, and give it a push in the right direction.

Culture — a canoe pointing towards the waterfall, the sandbar, the rocks — informs and reflects all aspects of life. Find opportunities for positive cultural exchanges. Invest in sustainable creativity. Establish symbiotic relationships. Cultivate collaboration.

SOURCE: Worldwatch Institute, 2000

SOURCE: Worldwatch Institute, 2000

1.
LOUISE MICHEL
(1830-1905, French)

"It is the people who will deliver us from the men who have been corrupting us, and the people themselves will win their liberty."

— Louise Michel, socialist, anarchist and schoolteacher active in the Paris Commune and the French Revolution of the 1870s. For her part in organizing an anarchist demonstration in Paris, she was sentenced to six years of solitary confinement, and ten years of police supervision. In her memoirs, she said: "It is not a question of breadcrumbs. What is at stake is the harvest of an entire world, a harvest necessary to the whole future human race, one without exploiters and without exploited." After her release from prison, while giving a speech, she was shot in an attempted assassination. She recovered and continued her activism.

"The story of social struggle throughout history is that defeats take place, but people persist. If there's fundamental grievance that remains, people may remain quiet for a while, but people ultimately will rise up against it and things will change." — **Howard Zinn**, historian

---

In **1835**, child workers in the silk mills in Paterson, New Jersey went on strike for the **11**-hour day.

In **1874**, as unemployed workers demonstrated in New York's Tompkins Square Park, a detachment of mounted police charged into the crowd, beating hundreds of men, women and children indiscriminately with billy clubs. The New York Commissioner of Police, Abram Duryee said: "It was the most glorious sight I ever saw..."

In **1877**, a general strike (because of wage cuts and poor working conditions) halted U.S. railways. Federal troops were called out to force an end to the nationwide strike. At the "Battle of the Viaduct" in Chicago, federal troops (recently returned from a massacre of Native Indians) killed **30** workers and wounded over **100**.

In **1887**, the Louisiana Militia shot **35** unarmed black sugar workers striking for a **$1** a day wage.

In **1888**, in London, matchgirls (women and teenage girls) went on strike prompted by the poor working conditions in their match factory including **14** hour work days, poor pay and the severe health complications of working with phosphorus, such as "phossy jaw", a medical condition where a deposit of phosphorus in the jaw bones would lead to painful toothaches and a swelling of the gums. The jawbone would begin to abscess, a process that was painful, disfiguring and foul-smelling. The jawbones would gradually rot away and turn a greenish-white colour that would glow in the dark. Removing the jawbones might save the person's life, otherwise they would die. Public outcry forced match manufacturers to change their process of manufacturing to eliminate "phossy jaw." But in some countries, reluctant companies had to be forced by legislation to make these changes. As for the London matchgirls, **3** weeks after beginning the strike, the factory owners capitulated.

In **1909**, female garment workers went on strike in New York which led to many arrests. A judge told those arrested: "You are on strike against God." After **4** months the strike ended when factory owners agreed to improve wages, working conditions, and hours.

In **1912**, women and children were beaten by police during a textile strike against the American Woolen Company in Lawrence, Massachusetts.

In **1914**, **5** men, **2** women and **12** children died as a result of a machine gun attack by company "guards," engaged by John D. Rockefeller, Jr. and other mine operators in an attempt to make strikers at Colorado's Ludlow Mine Field return to work.

In **1916**, strikebreakers hired by the Everett Mills owner attacked and beat strikers in Everett, Washington. Police watched and refused to intervene, claiming that the waterfront where the incident took place was Federal land and therefore outside their jurisdiction. Later, in response, the Industrial Workers of The World (IWW) called a union meeting, whereupon company gunman fired on union members, killing **7** and wounding **50**.

In **1917**, thousands of armed company vigilantes forced **1,185** mine workers in Bisbee, Arizona into manure-laden boxcars and "deported" them to the New Mexico desert. The workers had been striking for improved safety and working conditions at the copper mine, an end to discrimination against unions, the equal treatment of foreign and minority workers, and a fair wage.

In **1917**, in British Columbia, Ginger Goodwin would lead smelter workers in an unsuccessful strike for the **8**-hour day. A year later Goodwin would be assassinated by a private policeman. His funeral was marked by the province's first general strike.

In **1917**, after the threat of a national railway strike, the Supreme Court approved the **8**-Hour Day Act.

In **1920-21**, the struggle to unionize in West Virginia, led to a march by **10,000** armed miners that ended with the miners fighting state militia, local police, and mine guards. It was the largest insurrection the U.S. had seen since the Civil War. Army troops later defeated the miners.

In **1922**, during a coal mine strike at Herrin, Illinois, **36** miners were killed.

In **1933**, **4** workers are killed before a pay-hike is won by **18,000** striking cotton workers in Pixley, California.

In **1938**, in the U.S. the Wages and Hours Act is passed, banning child labour and setting the **40**-hour work week.

In **1952**, President Truman ordered the U.S. Army to seize the nation's steel mills to avert a strike. The act is later ruled illegal by the Supreme Court.

In **1970**, California grape growers sign an agreement after a **5**-year strike by the United Farm Workers.

In **1981**, Federal air traffic controllers began a nationwide strike. Most of the **13,000**-strikers defy a back-to-work order and are later fired by President Reagan.

In **2004**, during a strike by **5000** sugar mill workers and sugarcane farmers in Hacienda Luisita, Philippines, **14** people are killed by the army and police outside the company gates, including **2** children aged **2** and **5** years old who died from suffocation from teargas lobbed by the police and army dispersal teams. At least **35** people were reported to have sustained gunshot wounds, **133** were arrested and detained, hundreds were wounded and another hundred still missing.

As of **2006, 9** union leaders at Coca-Cola's bottling plants in Colombia have been murdered. Hundreds of other Coke workers have been tortured, kidnapped and/or illegally detained by violent paramilitaries, often working closely with plant management.

SOURCES: *Trade Unions of the World* (John Harper Publishing), *2005; American Labor Struggles* (Anchor Foundation), 1974; Carpenters Union of BC, 2006, KillerCoke.org, 2006; *The Encyclopedia of American Facts and Dates* (Harper Collins), 1997; allen lutins, 2005; *Labor Conflict in the United States: An Encyclopedia* (Garland Publishing), 1990; *The Samuel Gompers Papers* (U of Illinois Press), 1997.

The *gap* between the incomes of the richest and poorest countries was about

3 to **1** in **1820**,

35 to **1** in **1950**,

44 to **1** in **1973**,

and **72** to **1** in **1992**.

SOURCE: United Nations Development Report, 1999

In the 1990s, **13 million** children *died from diarrhea* (more than all the people in the world killed because of armed conflict since the Second *World War*).

SOURCE: United Nations, Guardian Weekly, 2003

The amount of money spent on

pet food

in the U.S. and Europe each year equals the
additional amount needed to provide
basic food and health care
for all the people in poor countries,
with a sizeable amount left over.

SOURCE: U.N. Human Development Report, 1999

Food bank use in Canada has increased
by **98%** since 1997.

SOURCE: Canadian Association of Food Banks,
Shared Vision Magazine, 2003

The amount of money spent on ICE cream
in Europe each year would be enough
to ensure reproductive health for **all women**
in developing countries per year.

SOURCE: United Nations Development Report, 1999

In the U.S. in 1998, almost

70% of wealth was in the hands of

10% of the population.

SOURCE: United for a Fair Economy, 2002

The U.S. has the *highest* rate of child poverty among the industrialized countries, with 1 in every **5 children** growing up in ***poverty.***

SOURCE: American Indicators website, 1997

Women and children make up

76% of *poor people* in the U.S.

SOURCE: Institute for Women's Policy Research, 2001

Goodie bags for **Oscar presenters** at the Academy Awards are worth **$100,000**.

SOURCE: Guardian Weekly, 2006

When U.S. Vice-President *Dick* Cheney was CEO of oil field supply company Halliburton, he did almost **$24 million** in business with *Saddam Hussein*.

SOURCE: Chicago Tribune, 2002

In the South American Andes, a company called **Barrick Gold Corporation** (through its subsidiaries) plans to destroy snow glaciers in order to extract gold, silver, copper and mercury in a open-pit strip mine. 1 of these snow glaciers in Pascua-Lama, Chile has nourished the region for thousands of years and destroying it would irreversibly damage the ecosystems and life of the indigenous (Diaguita) communities. Pascua-Lama's glaciers constitute a natural reserve for fresh water for the San Guillermo UNESCO World Heritage Biosphere site.

SOURCE: Mining Watch Canada website, 2005

1.1 billion

(**1/6** of the world's population)
do not have clean water.
2.4 billion do not have adequate sanitation.
1 child dies every **15** seconds from
water-related disease, which amounts to
nearly **6,000** deaths a day or the equivalent
of **20** jumbo jets crashing.

SOURCE: Guardian Weekly, 2004

The **$8 billion** spent on
cosmetics in the U.S. each year would provide
clean water for the developing world.

SOURCE: UN Human Development Report, 1999

The production costs of an hour of
"reality" TV programming is about

$800,000.

SOURCE: Globe and Mail, 2004

Global production of *hazardous waste*
has reached more than
300 million
tons a year.

SOURCE: Worldwatch Institute, Guardian Weekly, 2003

The **petrochemical** (oil) industry creates
materials used to produce **5 million**
different products including computers, textiles,
nylons and unbreakable toys.
5 effects on health from the release of
contaminants (during the making of chemicals
by the petrochemical industry) into the
atmosphere are allergies, asthma, leukemia,
cancer and genetic malformations.

SOURCE: Alerta Verde 144, Acción Ecológica, Oilwatch website, 2006

In the *Forbes 400* list of the richest people in the world, **5** of the top **10** were members of the Walton family, owners of Wal-Mart (worth **$18 billion** each).

SOURCE: Forbes, 2004

The average annual pay for a cashier at Wal-Mart is **$14,000**, **$1,000** below the federal poverty line for a family of **3**. Wal-Mart does not provide health insurance to over half of its **1.3** million U.S. employees. Wal-Mart admits **46%** of the children of Wal-Mart employees have no health coverage.

SOURCE: Wal-Mart Watch, 2005

Elizabeth Paige Laurie, an heiress to the Wal-Mart fortune, was under investigation at the University of Southern California over claims that she paid a fellow student **$20,000** to complete her coursework.

SOURCE: Guardian Weekly, 2004

In 2005, a group called **"Working Families for Wal-Mart"** was set up to let the public know how good Wal-Mart is at helping ordinary families. It turns out most of the group's money came from Wal-Mart.

SOURCE: The Times, London, 2006

In 2006, former U.S. Ambassador Andrew Young became spokesman for "Working Families for Wal-Mart," only to resign after admitting to making **"demagogic"** remarks about Jewish, Asian and Arab business owners. Herman Cain, a steering committee member of the group (WFFWM) said anyone critical of Wal-Mart are "Hezbocrats, a roaming band of militant guerrillas."

SOURCE: Center For Media and Democracy, 2006

In 2002, the Maquila Solidarity Network named both **Wal-Mart** and the **Hudson's Bay Company** "Sweatshop Retailers of the Year."

SOURCE: Ethical Trading Action Group, Shared Vision Magazine, 2003

Wal-Mart won a legal victory in Maryland, when a state law requiring larger retailers to provide workers minimal levels of **health insurance** was struck down.

SOURCE: Guardian Weekly, 2006

1 in every **5** meals

eaten in the US is *fast* food.

SOURCE: UTNE Reader, 2003

India's highest court ordered **Coca-Cola** to reveal its secret formula for the first time in **120 years**, after a chemical study found that **11** brands sold by the company contained unacceptable levels of insecticides.

SOURCE: The Times, London, 2006

Coke represents **10%** of the total liquids consumed in the world.

SOURCE: UTNE Reader, 2003

$13 billion

a year would satisfy the
world's sanitation and food needs
(about as much as the people of the U.S.
and European Union spend each year on
perfume).

SOURCE: Ignacio Ramonet, Le Monde Diplomatique, 1998

Nearly **1/2** of the food America
produces is wasted. The rate of loss, even
partially corrected, could save U.S.
consumers and corporations
tens of billions of dollars each year.

SOURCE: a study by Professor Timothy Jones, U of Arizona, 2004

Adolf Hitler's only book, **Mein Kampf**,
written before he became dictator of Germany
in 1933, has become a bestseller in Turkey.

SOURCE: Guardian Weekly, 2005

An estimated **50,000** *women*

and *children* are trafficked into the U.S. for sexual or forced labour every year.

SOURCE: U.S. Central Intelligence Agency, 2000

In Kosovo, women are bought and sold as sex slaves for up to

$3,500.

The sex slave industry has increased during the

last **5** years with help from western troops stationed there and local police.

SOURCE: Amnesty International, 2004

Madonna and Guy Ritchie's wedding cost between **$2** and **$3 million**.

SOURCE: USA Today, 2002

SOURCE: Bread For The World Institute, 2004

2.

EMMA GOLDMAN

(1869-1940, Lithuanian)

"Considered from this angle, I think my life and my work have been successful. What is generally regarded as success—acquisition of wealth, the capture of power or social prestige—I consider the most dismal failures. I hold when it is said of a man that he has arrived, it means that he is finished—his development has stopped at that point. I have always striven to remain in a state of flux and continued growth, and not to petrify in a niche of self-satisfaction."

— Emma Goldman, anarchist, lecturer, editor, protester. She fought countless battles for free speech and civil liberties. She critiqued the social and economic subordination of women and was an early advocate of birth control.

3

search engines (**Yahoo**, **Microsoft** and **Google**) have co-operated with China in preventing **123** million Chinese Internet users from having access to information about human rights abuses, according to Amnesty International (London) the companies "have violated their stated corporate values and policies" in their pursuit of China's booming Internet market. A.I. also says Yahoo passed on evidence about its users to authorities, including information that led to the prosecution of **2** Chinese journalists.

SOURCE: CBC Arts Report, 2006

Microsoft is suspected of being behind a deluge of readers' letters sent to newspapers complaining about the U.S. Justice Department's antitrust lawsuit against Microsoft in **2001**.

SOURCE: The Times, London, 2006

In Swaziland, life expectancy has fallen by **25** **years** since the spread of HIV.

In the countryside teenage girls sell sex for **$5**, exactly what it costs to

hire a pair of oxen for a day of ploughing.

SOURCE: Guardian Weekly, 2003

Life expectancy in Zimbabwe is
31 years (in the early 1970s it was **56**).
In Britain life expectancy *rose* from
72 to **78 years**.

SOURCE: United Nations, Guardian Weekly, 2003

2.3 million people died of AIDS in 2004 and
25.4 million were HIV-positive.

SOURCE: Guardian Weekly, 2005

Of the **4.4 billion** people in developing countries:

3/5 lack basic **sanitation**,

1/3 have no safe **drinking water**,

1/4 have inadequate **housing**,

1/5 are **undernourished**

1/5 have no modern **health services**.

SOURCE: United Nations Development Report, 1999

In 2003, British people spent more than
$2 billion on *candy*.

SOURCE: Guardian Weekly, 2003

20 million people in the world who need a wheelchair for basic mobility do not have **1**.

SOURCE: United Nations report, 2004

In India, gangs kidnap beggars and force them to have **limbs amputated** by doctors who receive about **$230** per operation. The value of the beggars is increased the fewer limbs they have.

SOURCE: Guardian Weekly, 2006

Globally the number **1** occupation for disabled people is begging.

SOURCE: Guardian Weekly, 2004

According to Texas-based Android World, Inc., Valerie, an attractive female-shaped robot can be purchased for **$59,000**. Valerie is expected to do all the owner's ironing and cleaning.

SOURCE: Guardian Weekly, 2004

It costs up to **$40,000** annually to provide temporary shelter and health services for a homeless person compared with **$28,000** a year to provide permanent housing to a formerly homeless person.

SOURCE: BC Government study by Prof. David Hulchanski, 2001.

1 million children in Canada live below the poverty line.

SOURCE: Campaign 2000 Report, 2004

100 million children in the world are estimated to be living or working on the streets and **1.2 million** women and girls under **18** are trafficked for prostitution each year.

SOURCE: United Nations, 2000

In the United Kingdom, **91%** of **12-year-olds** own a mobile phone.

SOURCE: Guardian Weekly, 2006

"Save Our Species Alliance" has been accused of being a front for timber lobbyists trying to weaken the U.S. **1973** Endangered Species Act. The group is headed by a veteran PR man and ex-president of the Oregon Forest Industries Council. In **2005**, he helped rewrite the Endangered Species Act, with the new act "widely denounced by environmentalists as a disturbing retreat from habitat protection and a paperwork nightmare for agencies seeking to revive the **1,268** threatened and endangered plants and animals in America, **186** of which are in California."

SOURCE: The Times, London, 2006

The **human race** is living beyond its means. A report backed by **1,360** scientists from **95** countries warned that almost **2/3** of the natural machinery that supports life on Earth is being degraded by human pressure.

SOURCE: Guardian Weekly, 2005

The **225** **richest people** in the world have a *combined* wealth of more than **$1 trillion**, equal to the annual *income* of the poorest **47%** of the Earth's population, some **2.5 billion people**.

SOURCE: United Nations Development Report, 1999

Former chief economist of the World Bank Joseph Stiglitz in his book "Making Globalisation Work" admits that **globalisation** makes some people poorer and that Africa has gotten poorer since the **1980s** while wages for the average American family have fallen as the U.S. continues to borrow **$2 billion** a day from the rest of the world.

SOURCE: The Observer, 2006

18,000 **people** died in the Bhopal, India explosion at a Union Carbide chemical plant in 1984. Survivors of the explosion continue to die at a rate of

1 a day.

Dow Chemical bought the plant in 2001 but refuses to accept responsibility for cleaning up the **5,000** tons of toxic waste left behind.

SOURCE: The Globe And Mail, 2004

The U.S. spends about

$19 billion annually on the

"war on drugs." A survey on the first year of George Bush's presidency, indicated *drug use* among young people had increased.

SOURCE: Guardian Weekly, 2002

Nearly **3,000 people** died
in the World Trade Center *attacks*
of Sept. 11, 2001. That same year
30,622 committed suicide and
700,142 died of heart disease in the U.S.

SOURCE: Globe & Mail, 2003

About **650,000** Iraqi civilians
(many of them women and children) have died
since the U.S.-led invasion according to the
Lancet medical journal.

SOURCE: Washington Post, 2006

The FBI and other U.S. law enforcement
agencies involved in counter-terrorism have
made over **200 requests** for
information about those who borrowed books
from the library system since **Sept. 11, 2001**,
including those who asked for a book on
Osama bin Laden.

SOURCE: Guardian Weekly, 2005

Average income of the heads of **12** publicly held *news* companies is **$3.6 million**.

SOURCE: American Journalism Review, 2000

In 2005, **37 million** Americans lived in poverty, **25.3%** were American Indians and Alaska Natives, **24.9%** were Blacks, **21.8%** were Hispanics, **11.1%** were Asians, and **8.3%** were Whites.

SOURCE: U.S. Census Bureau News, 2006

The **3** richest people in the world have assets that exceed the combined gross domestic product of the

48

least-*developed* countries.

SOURCE: United Nations Development Report, 1999

In Canada, they have a **public health care** system; in America they have a **private health care** system. In Canada, total health care spending is **$3,298 per person** and in America they spend over **$7,000 per person**. In Canada, all citizens have health care coverage; in America **1** in **7** citizens have no coverage. In Canada, life expectancy is rated **#2** in the world; in America life expectancy is rated **#25** in the world. In Canada, health professionals determine who receives care based on medical need; in America, insurance companies and the ability to pay decide access and treatment. In America, the Infant Mortality Rate is **40%** higher than in Canada.

SOURCE: Council of Canadians, 2006

The space shuttle costs **$400 million** per flight. NASA's *overall* budget is **$15 billion** a year.

SOURCE: Guardian Weekly, 2003

A child dies of starvation every

7 seconds according to the

World Food Programme.

SOURCE: Guardian Weekly, 2004

At **400,000** operations a year,

liposuction is now the leading form of

cosmetic surgery in the U.S.

SOURCE: Worldwatch Institute, 2000

Up to **24,000** people a day die of

hunger-related causes

in the African country of Malawi.

25%

of them are children.

SOURCE: John Vidal, Guardian Weekly, 2002

Nike has spent approximately

$60 million on advertising

campaigns featuring Spike Lee,
Michael Jordan, and others. According to a study
by the Girl Scouts of America,
Michael Jordan is one of the **3** living
Americans whom *kids most admire*.

SOURCE: Consumers Union, 1998

The Gap, in its **1**st
"social responsibility report"
admitted unsafe machinery and child labour
violations were widespread in thousands
of its factories.

SOURCE: Guardian Weekly, 2004

In **Uruguay**, **33%** of citizens have fallen below
the poverty line and **8%** live in extreme poverty.

SOURCE: Root Cause of Poverty in Latin America by Mario Osava, 2005

In Bangladesh, an estimated
500,000 children are *slaves*.

SOURCE: Bangladesh Bureau of Statistics, 1996

In the year 2000, **250,000** persons
were trafficked from Southeast Asia; **150,000**
from south Asia, **100,000** each from the
Russian Federation and Latin America; **75,000**
from Eastern Europe, and another **50,000** from
Africa. An estimated **35%** of all trafficked
persons globally are children
under the age of consent.

SOURCE: Women Aid International Press Release, 2003

Child poverty rates for Aboriginal, immigrant
and visible minority children are more than
2 times the average for all children in Canada.

SOURCE: Campaign 2000 Report, 2004

It would cost between

$7 and 8 billion a year to

provide primary *education* for everyone in the

developing world. This amount represents

4 days of global *military spending*, and

50% of what the U.S. spends annually

on *children's toys*.

SOURCE: Guardian Weekly, 1999

The Tax Justice Network says Britain, America
and Switzerland rank among the **3** most
corrupt countries in the world because of the
abuse of offshore tax havens by rich individuals.

SOURCE: Guardian Weekly, 2006

A Canadian study shows that the
wealthiest nations
do not have the healthiest people.
Instead, it is the countries with the
smallest economic gap
between **rich** and **poor**.

SOURCE: Mark Bourrie, Inter Press Service, 1999

Aid sent to the developing world can
sometimes be more effective if sent to state and
local governments (instead of the national
government). Historically, much foreign aid was

provided *not* to promote development but to

purchase friendship, especially during the cold
war. The West gave money to the **brutal
dictator Mobutu**, knowing it was going into
his Swiss bank accounts rather
than to the people of Zaire.

SOURCE: Guardian Weekly, 2005

In Sri Lanka, **10,000** children

are *enslaved* in brothels.

SOURCE: CATW, Coalition Report, 1997

America's second-biggest bank,
JP Morgan Chase, has apologized for the
involvement of its subsidiaries in the slave
trade **2 centuries** ago. The bank admitted that
it accepted slaves as loan collateral and
because of this it owned **several hundred**.
The bank apologized because it does
business with the City of Chicago which
requires companies to detail such dealings.

SOURCE: Guardian Weekly, 2005

80%

of the world's industrial output is
controlled by **1,000** corporations.

SOURCE: Andrew Lithgow, Shared Vision Magazine, 2003

There are more African-American males
in **prison** than enrolled in *colleges*
or *universities*.

SOURCE: New York Times, 2002

An analysis by *The Washington Post* of the
U.S. Department of Justice's terrorism
prosecutions has discovered only
39 out of **400 suspects** have actually
been convicted of terrorist related crimes
since **Sept 11, 2001.**

SOURCE: Guardian Weekly, 2005

Out of the **9** million prisoners in the world,

the U.S. *imprisons* nearly **2** million.

SOURCE: Home Office, Britain, 2003

3.
RUDOLPH ROCKER

(1873-1958, German)

"The portentous development of our present economic system, leading to a mighty accumulation of social wealth in the hands of privileged minorities and to a constant repression of the great masses of the people, prepared the way for the present political and social reaction and befriended it in every way. It sacrificed the general interests of human society to the private interests of individuals, and thus systematically undermined a true relationship between men. People forgot that industry is not an end in itself, but should be only a means to insure to man his material subsistence and to make accessible to him the blessings of a higher intellectual culture. Where industry is everything, where labour loses its ethical importance and man is nothing, there begins the realm of ruthless economic despotism, whose workings are no less disastrous than those of any political despotism."

— Rudolf Rocker, anarcho-syndicalist, labour organizer

Half of the world's population lives
on *less* than **$2** a day.

SOURCE: Paul Brown, Guardian Weekly, 2002

U.S. college students consume more than **4** billion cans of beer each year. Stacked on end, these cans would reach **120,000** miles beyond the moon.

SOURCE: http://www.uvm.edu/~naguiar/teach.html, 2004

In the entire world, those living in extreme poverty (on less than **$1 a day**) rose from **271 million** in **1996** to **313 million** in **2002**. That is an increase of **42 million** people in **6 years**.

SOURCE: Guardian Weekly, 2005

From 1990 to 2005, a CEO's salary increased almost **300%**, while a production worker's salary increased **4.3%**.

SOURCE: G. William Domhoff, University of California, Santa Cruz, 2006

1/3 of the world's population is *without* electricity. If present trends continue, this figure will grow by **25%** in the next **20** years.

SOURCE: Paul Brown, Guardian Weekly, 2002

For **$12** you can buy **"SPRAY ON MUD"** for your **SUV**. According to the company's website, SPRAY ON MUD can give the impression "you've just come back from a day's shooting, fishing, or visiting friends on a farm" instead of dropping the kids off at the mall on your way to yoga class. The creator of SPRAY ON MUD reassures us that "people may want to look like they've been off-road, but they certainly don't want any chips or scratches on paint work."

SOURCE: Guardian Weekly, 2005

In **2003**, fast food chain **KFC** began an ad campaign to portray its fried chicken as health food and useful in losing weight. The ads were pulled after a complaint to the Federal Trade Commission. One of the ads gave the impression that eating fried chicken was low in carbs and responsible for a man's **"fantastic"** looks. The ads did briefly flash a virtually illegible disclaimer that fried chicken is not a "low fat, low cholesterol, low sodium food."

SOURCE: Center for Science in the Public Interest, 2003

In 2004, an estimated
150,000
people in the U.S. will have stomach-shrinking surgery

costing about **$25,000** each.

SOURCE: The Washington Post, 2004

Second Harvest, the U.S.'s largest chain of food banks, provided food for almost

26 million people,

leaving **2.3 million** turned away.

SOURCE: American Indicators website, 1997

KFC is being sued over its use of partially hydrogenated oil, better known as trans fat, which is a contributing factor in the deaths of roughly **50,000** Americans every year. The class action suit asks that the court prohibit KFC from using trans fat or, at least, post signs in KFCs saying many of their foods are high in trans fat. A typical **3-piece Extra Crispy combo meal** (drumstick, **2** thighs, potato wedges, **1** biscuit) has **15** grams of trans fat; more than a person should consume in **1** week. Trans fat is more harmful than saturated fat, since it raises one's LDL cholesterol (bad), and lowers HDL cholesterol (good).

SOURCE: Center for Science in the Public Interest, 2006

McDonald's promised to reduce trans fat in cooking oil in **2002**, but it reneged on that promise in **2003**. In **2004**, California trial attorney Stephen Joseph filed a lawsuit against McDonald's over its broken promise, which the company settled in **2005** by agreeing to pay **$7 million** to the American Heart Association. McDonald's still has not changed its oil.

SOURCE: Center for Science in the Public Interest, 2006

Wendy's fast-food chain has switched to a non-hydrogenated mixture of corn and soybean oil in its deep-fryers, making its fried foods virtually trans-fat-free. The **700**-outlet Ruby Tuesday chain has dumped partially hydrogenated oil (in favour of canola oil).

SOURCE: Center for Science in the Public Interest, 2006

In **Argentina**, the rate of poverty rose from **22.6%** to **54%** between 1992 and 2002.

SOURCE: Root Cause of Poverty in Latin America by Mario Osava, 2005

Europe and the U.S. subsidize their farmers by **$350 billion** a year (more than **6** times what they spend on aid to poor countries). This allows western farmers to flood food cheaply into poor countries, depress prices and undermine local farming. **20** years ago, Ghana exported rice; today its rice industry has collapsed. Under U.S. and Thai exports, **20%** of Africa's food *now* comes from rich countries, though it *could* grow its own.

SOURCE: John Vidal, Guardian Weekly, 2002

In **Communist China**, factory workers who make running shoes for a major North American firm, get paid **$2.50 a day** and work **60 hours** a week. The workers live under military-style discipline and are fined for any attempt to organize to improve their conditions.

SOURCE: Vancouver Sun, 2006

Only **10%** of the **$70** billion spent on *developing* new drugs each year is devoted to the diseases that cause **90%** of the world's *health problems*.

SOURCE: Guardian Weekly, 2003

In 2004, at a hearing before the U.S. Senate Finance Committee, pharmaceutical company **Merck** was forced to explain why it had waited **5 years** to take its drug Vioxx (with profits of **$2.5 billion** a year) off the market when an estimated **139,000** Americans had already suffered serious side effects, many of them fatal. Merck knew of the potential problems as early as 1999. Vioxx is a medicine used to relieve arthritis, acute pain in adults, and painful menstrual cycles.

SOURCE: Weitz & Luxenberg, 2004

"In the largest criminal tax case ever filed, **KPMG** (a global network of firms providing audit, tax, and advisory services) has admitted that it engaged in a fraud that generated at least **$11 billion** in phony tax losses which, according to court papers, cost the United States at least **$2.5 billion** in evaded taxes."

SOURCE: U.S. Justice Department, 2005

In the U.S., energy, mining, and waste management industries contributed **$29.7 million** to political campaigns in 1999–2000, and spent another **$159 million** on direct lobbying activities in 2000 to coax decision-makers to favour corporate interests.

SOURCE: Center for Responsive Politics, 2003

Enron, once the **7th** largest company in the U.S., paid *no income tax* between 1996 and 1999.

SOURCE: Guardian Weekly, 2003

In the world, approximately **5,000** women and girls a year are victims of "honour killings" by family members (female relatives are killed for activities that the family feels dishonours their reputation by perceived misuse of sexuality). "Honour killings" have been reported in **Bangladesh**, **Brazil**, **Ecuador**, **Egypt**, **India**, **Israel**, **Italy**, **Jordan**, **Morocco**, **Pakistan**, **Sweden**, **Turkey**, **Uganda** and the **United Kingdom**.

SOURCE: United Nations Population Fund, 2000

In the U.S., a woman is raped every

6 minutes.

SOURCE: www.amnestyusa.org/women, 2004

The chance of a woman in **Sweden** dying in childbirth is **1** in **29,800** while in **Niger** it is **1** in **7**.

SOURCE: Guardian Weekly, 2006

The U.S. *defence* budget in 2005 was over

$1 billion a day.

SOURCE: New Routes: A Journal of Peace Research & Action, 2005

DAILY DEATHS around the world:
24,000 from hunger
6,000 children from diarrhea
2,700 children from measles
1,400 women in childbirth
550 children from war
201 from drought

SOURCE: American Indicators website, 2003

For many of the world's poorest countries, living standards are *lower* than what they were

30 years ago.

SOURCE: Charlotte Denny, Guardian Weekly, 2002

Every **4** days the world *spends* more than

$7 billion on the military.

The U.N. estimates that this amount would be enough to provide poor countries with primary *education* for a year.

SOURCE: Charlotte Denny, Guardian Weekly, 2002

The military involvement in Afghanistan and Iraq have cost the U.S. **$400 billion** in **3** years.

SOURCE: Guardian Weekly, 2006

The **U.S. military** estimates it will take **70** years to clean up its *contamination* of thousands of properties it once owned, at a cost of **$20 billion**.

SOURCE: New York Times, 2002

U.S. states vying for federal **"anti-terrorism"** contract money include Indiana which has identified **8,591** potential terrorism targets including a corn farm in a district populated by horse-drawn-buggy driving Amish.

SOURCE: The Observer, 2006

In 2006, **90** officials

of the U.S. Department of Homeland Security have left the department to make money in the anti-terrorism industry as lobbyists and consultants.

SOURCE: The Observer, 2006

Software company Dulles Research, claims its technology can detect terrorists by monitoring everyday behaviour such as travel schedules, credit card usage and bank transfers. It is now bidding for a government contract to monitor millions of people for suspicious patterns.

SOURCE: The Observer, 2006

When the scandal of the **Nike** sweatshops broke in 1996, Nike workers in Vietnam were earning **20 cents** an hour. That same year, Tiger Woods had his first Nike contract for **$40 million**. If he worked *every* single day for the **5 years** of his contract, he would be earning **$2,739.73** an hour.

SOURCE: Montreal Gazette, 2001

A video on YouTube critiquing Al Gore and his film about the dangers of global warming was credited to a **29-year-old** from Beverly Hills who was in fact a guy from a PR company called DCI Group based in Washington, DC. Among the PR company's clients are oil multinational **ExxonMobil**. DCI Group also operates a news and opinion website sponsored by ExxonMobil, General Motors and McDonald's which offers a highly skeptical view of climate change.

SOURCE: The Wall Street Journal, 2006

In 1989, the Exxon Valdez spilled over **30 million** gallons of crude oil into Alaska's Prince William Sound. The spill covered over **10,000 square miles** of coastal ocean and more than **3,200 miles** of shoreline, including **3** national parks, **4** national wildlife refuges, **1** national forest, **5** state parks, **4** state critical habitat areas, **1** state game sanctuary and in the process killed **250,000** birds, **2,800** sea otters, and **300** harbor seals. The herring fishery would later collapse and never recover. Many cleanup workers, after wading all day through the oil spill, would come home and find their urine was black. Some are still suffering chronic health effects. In 1994 a jury ordered Exxon to pay punitive damages of **$5 billion**. Seventeen years later Exxon has yet to pay

$1.

SOURCE: Pay up Exxon.org, 2006

The increased demand for **palm oil** (food manufacturers are replacing hydrogenated oils with palm oil in cookies, crackers, cereals, and microwave popcorn) is causing destruction of the rainforest habitats of Sumatran and Bornean orangutans, pushing them closer to extinction. Much of the demand for palm oil is being supplied by growers in Malaysia and Indonesia, whose authoritarian regimes care little about environmental destruction. When a rainforest is destroyed for plantations, the orangutans have less room to roam and reproduce and are targets for poachers. Borneo's orangutans were reduced by **1/3rd** in **1997**, when almost **8,000** were burned to death or killed as they fled fires set to clear rainforest for plantations. Products with non-hydrogenated soybean, corn, canola, or peanut oils are more environmentally friendly and better for human hearts and arteries than palm oil.

SOURCE: Center for Science in the Public Interest, 2006

113 **million** children in developing countries are *without* access to basic education. **60%** are girls.

SOURCE: Bread for the World Institute, 2002

In 2004, the **2** candidates (Democratic and Republican) spent an estimated total of

$1 billion

in the campaign to become **president** of the United States.

SOURCE: Globe and Mail, 2004

The amount of money that the *richest*

1% of the world's population makes each

year equals what the *poorest* **57%**

make.

SOURCE: Bread for the World Institute, 2003

A birthday party for former Tyco chief executive
Dennis Kozlowski's wife Karen, cost
$2.2 million. It included an ice sculpture of
Michelangelo's David that urinated vodka.

SOURCE: Guardian Weekly, 2004

Almost **2/3** of U.S.
companies paid no tax between
1996 and 2000.

SOURCE: General accounting office report, U.S. Congress, 2004

In India, it is estimated that more than

5,000

women are killed each year because their in-laws consider their dowries inadequate. Only a tiny percentage of their murderers are brought to justice.

SOURCE: United Nations, 2002

In Nigeria, girls and women are **trafficked** for forced prostitution to Italy, France, Spain, the Netherlands, Cote d'Ivoire, and Benin. Children are trafficked for involuntary domestic and agricultural labour and street peddling in West and Central Africa.

SOURCE: The Bureau of Democracy, U.S. State Department

The NY Times reported that the cost to film companies of campaigning to win an Oscar for their movies in **2002** was **$50 million** (**$137,000 a day** for a year).

SOURCE: The Observer, 2000

The United Nations estimates the cost of *combating* AIDS to be

$10 billion a year.

U.N. member countries contributed

$3 billion in 2002.

SOURCE: Guardian Weekly, 2002

In sub-Saharan Africa, **30** million people are *likely to die of HIV-related causes.*

Currently **300,000**

receive life-saving drugs.

SOURCE: Guardian Weekly, 2002

The **coffee** industry is worth **2** times what it was in 1990. But coffee bean farmers in the developing world *now receive* **50%** of the money they did in 1990.

SOURCE: Charlotte Denny, Guardian Weekly, 2002

Freedom Tobacco International Inc is offering a *lifetime supply* of cigarettes to **celebrity smokers** as part of a marketing campaign to raise the public profile of its recently launched brand.

SOURCE: Associated Press, 2003

In the world, every **8** seconds a person dies of a tobacco-related disease.

SOURCE: www.quite.org.au, 2003

"We're spending on Iraq and Afghanistan, something in the vicinity of

$9.5 billion U.S. a month. And

that's *more in one month in 2006* than we spent with the entire year of 2005 on AIDS."

SOURCE: Stephen Lewis, Georgia Straight, from statistics from the
Congressional Research Service, 2006

In the U.S. in **1999** there were **9 companies** with federal homeland security contracts. By **2003** it was **3,512**. In **2006**, there were **33,890** homeland security contracts. Since **2000**, **$130 billion** in contracts have been handed out.

SOURCE: The Observer, 2006

4 public bodies in Britain that invest in the arms trade are churches, universities, trade unions and charities.

SOURCE: The Campaign Against the Arms Trade, 2004

75%

of the world's *pollution* comes from

25% of the world's *population*.

SOURCE: Eduardo Galeano, Guardian Weekly, 2002

In a country of **200 million** cars,
President George Bush announced that U.S.
production of *greenhouse gases* will rise

43% by the year 2020.

SOURCE: Eduardo Galeano, Guardian Weekly, 2002

During George Bush's presidency,
polluting companies in the U.S. are paying

64% less in fines every month.

SOURCE: Guardian Weekly, 2003

26 major publications refused to run an
advertisement critical of **Victoria's Secret**.
The ad claimed that the **lingerie** retailer's
printing of over a million catalogs a day contributed to the destruction of North America's Great
Boreal Forest. Publications refusing to run the
ad included Rolling Stone, Marie Claire,
Lucky, BlackBook, and Nylon.
Premiere and **Paste** *did* run the ad.

SOURCE: Forest Ethics.org, 2006

In 1932, the original fashionista, **Hugo Boss**,
designed the uniforms worn by Hitler's SS
in **Nazi Germany**. The dapper black uniforms
sported a hot collar with silver flashes and
was topped off by a hat sporting a
silver death's-head. After the war the company
was labelled an "opportunist of the Third Reich."
Today, it has over **5,000** stores worldwide.

SOURCE: The Master Plan by Heather Pringle, 2006

An estimated **135** million of the world's girls and women have undergone genital mutilation, and **2** million girls a year are at risk of mutilation—approximately **6,000** per day.

SOURCE: Amnesty International, 2004

Average cost of cosmetic surgery in Canada:
Liposuction: **$2,000** per area
Breast lift: **$6,000**
Tummy tuck: **$5,000**
Face lift: **$8,000**
Brow lift: **$4,000**
Laser resurfacing (full face): **$4,000**
Botox injection: **$500**

SOURCE: Canadian Society for Aesthetic (Cosmetic) Plastic Surgery, 2004

4.

VOLTAIRINE DE CLEYRE

(1866-1912, American)

"If society were so constituted as to allow every man, woman and child to lead a normal life there would be no violence in this world. It fills me with horror to think of the brutal acts done in the name of government. Every act of violence finds its echo in another act of violence."

—Voltairine de Cleyre was an activist, writer and lecturer who lived much of her life in poverty. She advocated for economic independence for women, birth control, and sex education. Her life was a revolt against the system of male domination and the tyranny of exploitation. At the age of 36, she was wounded by a would-be assassin's bullet.

A ticket bought online at **Ticketmaster** for a John Mellencamp concert in Indiana was **$67.50**. Service charges included: **$10** convenience charge, **$2** processing fee and **$20** delivery fee. This **$67.50** ticket turned into nearly **$100** (a surcharge of almost **50%** of the face value of the ticket). **John Mellencamp** said "If you think it's just Ticketmaster that's doing that to the American people, you're crazy. It's every one of these stinking corporations. Every one of them."

SOURCE: Wish-TV, 2005

Since 1990, when **Chile**'s **17-year right wing** military dictatorship came to an end, the poverty rate has dropped from **38.5%** to **18.8%**.
The proportion of Chileans living in extreme poverty fell from **12.9%** to **4.7%** over the same period.

SOURCE: Root Cause of Poverty in Latin America by Mario Osava, 2005

If women in the U.S. earned the same amount as men, each family with a *woman working* outside the home, would have an increase of over **$4,000** in their *annual* household income.

SOURCE: Institute for Women's Policy Research, 2001

An analysis of **63 nations** found that improvements in *women's* education, healthcare and living standards were responsible for a **75%** reduction in their children's *malnutrition*.

SOURCE: Worldwatch Institute, 2000

1/6 of the world's population lives in squalid unhealthy areas mostly without water, sanitation, public services or legal security.

SOURCE: U.N. Settlements Report, Nairobi, 2003

Polling company Zogby International asked American voters in 2004, what the most urgent moral crisis in the U.S. was: **33%** said "greed and materialism." **31%** said "poverty and economic justice." Ranked well back at **16%** and **12%** respectively was "abortion" and "gay marriage."

SOURCE: Americans United, 2004

In the 1960s, children aged **2** to **14** directly influenced about **$5 billion** in parental purchases. In the mid-1970s, the figure was **$20 billion**, in 1984 it was **$50 billion**, in 1990 it was **$132 billion**. In 1997 it was close to **$188 billion**.

SOURCE: Psychologists Challenge Ethics Of Marketing To Children by Miriam Zoll, 2000

The *literacy* of adult Americans

ranks **10th** out of **17**

industrialized nations.

SOURCE: Business Week, 2002

The typical U.S. home averages

3 TVs, **3** radios, **2** VCRs, **2** CD players,

a video game player, a computer, as well as
newspapers, magazines and comic books.
Children are less likely to live in a home with just

1 TV, than in a house with **5** or more TVs.

SOURCE: The Kaiser Family Foundations, 1999

In Bangladesh, a lack of safe water
and poor hygiene kill hundreds of children
a day under the age of **5**.

SOURCE: Guardian Weekly, 2006

In 1970, the *average* American *CEO*

made **40** times the average worker's salary.

In 1998, the average American CEO

made **1,000** times

the *average worker's* salary.

SOURCE: Guardian Weekly, 2003

The United Nations budget
is less than
the yearly cost of the
Tokyo fire department.

SOURCE: American Indicators website, 1998

Average National Basketball Association
salary: **$3,522,134**

SOURCE: sportsfansofamerica.com, 2003

Over their *lifetime*,

1 **child** born in the West will consume and

pollute more than would **30** **children**

born in *developing* countries.

SOURCE: Paul Brown, Guardian Weekly, 2002

Children in the U.S. spend so many hours

watching **television**,

and playing *video* games, that "media user"

could qualify as their full-time job.

SOURCE: The Kaiser Family Foundations, 2003

52

of the *largest* economies
in the world are
corporate economies.

SOURCE: Andrew Lithgow, Shared Vision Magazine, 2003

At the City University of New York (CUNY),
the U.S.'s largest urban public university
(**450,000 students** on over **20** campuses),
has removed all **Coca-Cola** vending machines
from **2** of its campuses. This was a result of an
anti-Coke campaign supported by the student
government and the union that represents
faculty and staff.

SOURCE: KillerCoke.org, 2006

Due to *declining revenues* in the U.S.,
McDonald's only opened up

300 new restaurants in 2002,

compared with **1,100** in 1995.

A study in France found 4 to 7-year olds left
most of their Happy Meals *uneaten*. The
real attraction was the free toy that came with it.

SOURCE: Guardian Weekly, 2002

In 1993, Tobacco maker **Phillip Morris**
decided to create a grassroots citizens group
called "The Advancement of Sound Science
Coalition" to fight regulation of the tobacco
industry and to portray the
dangers of smoking as unfounded.

SOURCE: Guardian Weekly, 2006

Switching from an average car to a
four-wheel drive uses as much energy in
12 months as leaving your TV on for
28 years.

SOURCE: Sierra Club, 2004

In 2006, Canadians will spend **$1.15 billion**
on Halloween items such as candy, pumpkins,
costumes and decorations.

SOURCE: Retail Council of Canada, 2006

In 2002, **Glaxo Smith Kline** sold more than
2 million prescriptions (worth **$55 million**)
for PAXIL to treat mood disorders and
depression in U.S. children and adolescents.
The drug company was charged in 2004 with
suppressing **4** studies showing PAXIL to be
no more effective than a placebo
and at worst harmful.

SOURCE: Guardian Weekly, 2004

40 **million people**

in the world live with AIDS.

75% of them *live* in

sub-Saharan Africa.

SOURCE: Bread for the World Institute, 2002

In Orange County, CA, for **$260** a month, **"The Poop Butler Pooper Scooper"** will take care of your entire yard's dog poop on a prescheduled, routine basis so you never have to scoop it ever again. They will scoop all the dog poop your dog leaves behind in a professional manner and leave the dog poop in your trash. The Poop Butler also asks you to please keep an eye on your yard for the first few weeks to guarantee that none of your dog's favourite poop places have been overlooked.

SOURCE: Poop Butler.com, 2006

Follow-up studies after the Exxon Valdez spilled **11 million** gallons of crude oil in 1989 show that oil spills cause **100** times more damage than *previously* thought.

SOURCE: Guardian Weekly, 2002

The world's most profitable corporation, **ExxonMobil** has sales that amount to more than **$1 billion** a day. The company has used some of this money to contribute to **124** organizations that deny climate change.

SOURCE: Guardian Weekly, 2006

It takes **11,000 litres** of water to create **1** quarter-pounder hamburger.

SOURCE: Guardian Weekly, 2006

IG Farben was a German conglomerate of companies that manufactured **Zyklon B**, a poison used in gas chambers to kill millions of people for the Nazis during World War II. In 1941, an investigation found IG Farben had close relations with U.S. companies Standard Oil and duPont. When World War II ended, IG Farben was found guilty of war crimes and dismantled leaving members of the conglomerate, such as **Agfa**, **BASF** and **Bayer**, to continue long successful lives in business.

SOURCE: *The Crime and Punishment of IG Farben* by Joseph Borkin, 1978

"The action of **IG Farben** along with other industrialists in rallying to the support of Hitler at that time was undoubtedly a factor contributing to the seizure and consolidation of power by **Hitler**."

SOURCE: Nuernberg Military Tribunal, Volume VIII, Page 1245

President George Bush's grandfather, U.S. senator **Prescott Bush**, was a director and shareholder of companies that profited from their involvement with the financial backers (such as **IG Farben**) of Nazi Germany. Prescott Bush continued working with Nazi Germany until 1942, when his company's assets were seized under the Trading with the Enemy Act.

SOURCE: The Guardian, 2004

Since assuming power, President George Bush has disobeyed at least **740 laws**.

SOURCE: The Observer, 2006

Virginia-based **military firm** Select Armour, (with the knowledge of the CIA) is just **1 firm** planning to run covert military operations inside Somalia, contrary to a United Nations ruling.

SOURCE: Guardian Weekly, 2006

Glaxo Smith Kline has been cited in a lawsuit by the California attorney general accusing the pharmaceutical company of defrauding the state's benefit system for the poor, elderly and disabled of "potentially hundreds of millions of dollars."

SOURCE: Guardian Weekly, 2005

Maintaining the *current level* of poverty among migrant farmworkers saves the average U.S. household **$50** a year.

SOURCE: Eric Schlosser, Guardian Weekly, 2003

Poor people suffer greater housing shortages and lose their civil liberties in cities that host the **Olympics** according to Helen Jefferson Lenskyj, a sociologist from the University of Toronto and author of **2** books on the Olympics.

SOURCE: Georgia Straight, 2006

Noxious gasses emanating from waste illegally dumped off the Ivory Coast by a tanker registered to the company Trafigura Beheer in the Netherlands killed **3 people** and made **5,000 sick**.

SOURCE: Le Monde, 2006

In Colombia, "homemade landmines" can be made for **$3** but removing them can cost **$1,000**.

There are an estimated **100,000** landmines in Colombia.

SOURCE: Colombian Campaign to Ban Landmines, 2004

It costs between **$200 million** and **$1 billion** to *decommission* a nuclear reactor in Europe.

SOURCE: Guardian Weekly, 2002

The *richest* countries are home to
20% of the world's population

who consume **86%** of all resources.

SOURCE: Paul Brown, Guardian Weekly, 2002

After several failed tests, the Pentagon's **$100 billion** *(to date)* star wars missile defense system has finally destroyed

1 mock warhead.

SOURCE: Guardian Weekly, 2006

Oxfam estimates that to meet the health, education and sanitation target of the United Nations Millennium Development Goals would require **$48 billion** more in aid a year. Annual global military spending is **$953 billion**.

SOURCE: Guardian Weekly, 2006

Carbon monoxide *emissions* have risen
10% since the Climate Change Convention
was *signed* by **150** countries in
Rio De Janeiro, in **1992**.

SOURCE: Paul Brown, Guardian Weekly, 2002

Reducing poverty and disease in Africa is
unattainable without making biodiversity and its
socioeconomic value the foundation for
development policies according to the
Madagascar Declaration at the Conservation
International symposium.

SOURCE: Guardian Weekly, 2006

In British Columbia, a government study
showed that taxpayers saved about

$12,000 a year for every **homeless**

person moved into housing.

SOURCE: Globe & Mail, 2006

An average European *COW* receives

$2.20 a day

from the taxpayer in subsidies and other aid.

SOURCE: Charlotte Denny, Guardian Weekly, 2002

The average wedding in Canada costs
$20,000. In **2002**, Canadian couples spent
$4 billion on weddings.

SOURCE: Vancouver Courier, 2006

In New York, the average cost to taxpayers for
each **homeless person** is **$40,000** a
year (mostly from hospital services) while the
cost to taxpayers of providing a homeless
person with housing was about
$18,000 a year.

SOURCE: Globe & Mail, 2006

In 2002, the U.S. granted Poland
an interest-free loan of almost

$4 billion

to purchase *fighter* jets.

SOURCE: New York Times, 2002

Americans per capita *give* **$33** a year

for foreign aid, the **3rd** lowest of

22 donor countries.

Denmark gives **$326** per capita.

SOURCE: American Indicators website, 2001

Research shows that
community-based efforts,
whether in a small village or a large city,
are most *effective* in meeting
people's needs.

SOURCE: World Health Organisation, 1996

Nike's *income* from golf products rose from

$40 million in 1995
to $300 million in 2000.

SOURCE: Montreal Gazette, 2001

In the U.S., women earn

77 cents for every $1 a man does.

SOURCE: Forbes Online, 2004

Named in a survey by the London-based Economist Magazine in 2006 as the **best city** in the world to live for the **4th** straight year, Vancouver, Canada has also doubled its number of homeless people to **1,300** in the last **3 years**.

SOURCE: Greater Vancouver Regional District report, 2006

The National Council of Welfare report states that **welfare rates** in Canada were at their lowest in **19 years**. In Canada's richest province, Alberta (on track to its **13th** year of surplus budgets), a single person on welfare in **1986**, received roughly **$10,000** a year, but in **2005** it was **$5,050** a year.

SOURCE: The Dominion, 2006

Lord Conrad Black and his wife Barbara Amiel once charged **$24,950** for "summer drinks" to his former company Hollinger International.

SOURCE: Guardian Weekly, 2004

In 1999, and 2000, Carnival Cruise Line earned profits of approximately **$1 billion**, but paid virtually *no* corporate income tax.

SOURCE: Cruise Ship Blues (New Society), 2003

A *janitor* employed by Carnival Cruise Line makes less than **$1.55** an hour.

SOURCE: Cruise Ship Blues (New Society), 2003

In Swaziland,
the government agreed to buy the king
a *new jet* for
$60 million
(*twice* the country's annual health budget).

SOURCE: Guardian Weekly, 2003

Bechtel, a construction company
that traditionally supports the
U.S. Republican party, was awarded a

$34 million

contract to take part in rebuilding
Iraq's infrastructure after the U.S.-led war.

SOURCE: Guardian Weekly, 2003

Auditors have uncovered **$1.4 billion**
in questionable overcharging by **Halliburton**,
the U.S. military's biggest contractor in Iraq.
Former employees accused the company of
double billing on meals, grossly inflating the
prices of services and allowing soldiers to
bathe in contaminated water. The company's
original contract with the U.S. military was for
$16.4 billion.

SOURCE: Washington Post, 2006

In the U.S. an estimated

7 to 8 million people are homeless.

SOURCE: American Indicators website, 2000

U.S. census figures indicate that poverty
has risen by **7%** since George Bush assumed
power. Statistics also showed that the **10** states
with the lowest household income and where
people are less likely to have health care and
are most likely to live in poverty all voted
Republican in the presidential election of **2004**.

SOURCE: Guardian Weekly, 2006

Michael Eisner, CEO of **Disney**, makes **$9,783**
an hour compared with a Haitian worker who
stitches Disney products for **28 cents** an hour.

SOURCE: Katharine Viner, The Guardian, 2000

In **Brazil**, transferring **5%** of the income of the **wealthiest 20%** of the population to the **poorest 20%** would reduce the poverty rate from **22%** to **7%** according to the 2005 United Nations Human Development Report. This would then lift **26 million** people from below the poverty line. Brazil has the most unequal distribution of wealth in the world.

SOURCE: Root Cause of Poverty in Latin America by Mario Osava, 2005

Top 13 dead celebrities
who collectively earned
$247 million in the past **6** months:
1. Kurt Cobain **2**. Elvis Presley
3. Charles M. Schulz **4**. John Lennon
5. Albert Einstein **6**. Andy Warhol
7. Theodor Geisel (Dr. Seuss) **8**. Ray Charles
9. Marilyn Monroe **10**. Johnny Cash
11. J. R. R. Tolkien **12**. George Harrison
13.Bob Marley

SOURCE: Forbes Magazine, 2006

7 people who did not fit into the market place of their time:

Confucius (551-479 BC), a Chinese scholar whose work went unrecognized in his lifetime, yet 2,500 years later his writings are still studied.

William Blake (1757-1827), a British poet and painter who lived mostly in near poverty. He was buried, largely forgotten, in a dissenters' burial ground, but is now regarded as one of Britain's most significant poets and artists.

Franz Schubert (1797-1828), an Austrian composer whose music went unacknowledged in his lifetime, receiving only encouragement from his closest friends.

Vincent van Gogh (1853-1869), a Dutch painter who, it is believed, died having only ever sold 1 of his 900 paintings. The painting was called *The Red Vineyard* and it is rumored he worked on it for 10 years.

Charles Ives (1874-1954), an American businessman and composer whose music was largely ignored during his lifetime. For many years his works went unperformed, yet in time he would become known as one of the most important and original composers of the 20th century.

Zora Neale Hurston (1891-1960), an African-American who, unable to make a living with her writing, worked as a librarian and a maid. She died in a welfare home and was buried in an unmarked grave. Her work was rediscovered to great acclaim in the late 1960s.

Franz Kafka (1883-1924), Czechoslovakian writer who made his living working as a clerk in an insurance company until his tuberculosis forced him to retire. During his lifetime he published only 6 stories while none of his novels were published. He is now considered to be one of the greatest writers of the last century.

FURTHER INSPIRATION

"What can we do? We can reinvent civil disobedience in a million different ways. In other words, we can come up with a million ways of becoming a collective pain in the ass."

"Our strategy should be not only to confront empire but to lay siege to it. To deprive it of oxygen. To shame it. To mock it. With our art, our music, our literature, our stubbornness, our joy, our brilliance, our sheer relentlessness—and our ability to tell our own stories. Stories that are different from the ones we're being brainwashed to believe. The corporate revolution will collapse if we refuse to buy what they are selling—their ideas, their version of history, their wars, their weapons, their notion of inevitability. Remember this: We be many and they be few. They need us more than we need them."

— **Arundhati Roy,** novelist, 2003

9
SMALL ACTS
TO BEGIN CHANGING THE WORLD:

1. Join consumer boycotts and anti-sweatshop campaigns.
2. Organize cultural events that raise money for, and awareness of, groups fighting poverty.
3. Start a creative protest that no one has thought of.
4. Convince skilled and talented people to work on the problems confronting those in poverty.
5. Research what the poor need and do it.
6. Produce guerrilla theatre and radical cheerleading.
7. Engage in civil disobedience.
8. Buy fair trade products.
9. Hold a vigil.

"First they ignore you. Then they laugh at you. Then they fight you. Then you win."
— **Mahatma Gandhi (1869-1948)**

WESTERN NATIONS
THAT
HAVE SIGNIFICANTLY
REDUCED CHILD & FAMILY POVERTY
HAVE DONE SO BY:

1. Investing in early learning programs.
2. Childcare programs.
3. Increased childcare benefits.
4. National affordable housing programs.
5. Increased unemployment benefits.
6. An adequate minimum wage *(in North America that would be $10 an hour).*

SOURCE: Campaign 2000, 2004

"True compassion is more than flinging a coin to a beggar. It comes to see that an edifice which produces beggars needs restructuring."— **Martin Luther King, 1967**

6
SHORT STORIES
OF POSITIVE ACTION
& SOCIAL CHANGE:

At Cambridge University, Dr. Helen Lee developed a test for diseases such as HIV, chlamydia and trachoma that is inexpensive, fast and requires no refrigeration—which is essential for doctors working in the hot climates of developing countries.

SOURCE: The Guardian Weekly, 2006

The *Federation of Slum and Shackdwellers* makes positive changes to the third of the world's population who inhabit slums.   SOURCE: The Guardian, 2004

In Kenya, a group of women cast out of their village after being raped, formed a women-only village whose matriarch was invited to speak at the United Nations on gender empowerment.

SOURCE: Washington Post, 2005

Helen Ditsebe-Mhone of Botswana was awarded the 2003 *Poverty Eradication* prize by the United Nations for creating "an international model of how to support those living with HIV/AIDS and their communities."

SOURCE: United Nations Population Fund, 2004

In Sudan, with the help of an aid group, the Dinka tribe started a village seed bank to increase the amount of food they can grow. Aid groups have also provided loans for beehives as well as tools to turn metal from swords and tanks into fishhooks, knives and implements for ploughing. SOURCE: The Guardian, 2004

Brendan Baker of Vancouver, Canada joined *Engineers Without Borders* and went to Senegal to help local farmers develop technology for processing and selling cashews. He also helped develop pumps for cleaner drinking water.

SOURCE: The International Development Research Centre, 2006

CONNECT TO CHANGE:

DOCTORS WITHOUT BORDERS: emergency aid to victims of armed conflict, epidemics, and natural and human-made disasters. **www.doctorswithoutborders.org**

RECLAIM DEMOCRACY: works to restore citizen authority over corporations. **www.reclaimdemocracy.org**

AMNESTY INTERNATIONAL: a worldwide movement of people who campaign for internationally recognized human rights. **www.amnesty.org**

FAIR TRADE FEDERATION: an association of fair trade wholesalers, retailers, and producers whose members are committed to providing fair wages and good employment opportunities to economically disadvantaged artisans and farmers worldwide. **www.fairtradefederation.com**

GLOBAL EXCHANGE: advocates for global fair trade. **www.globalexchange.org**

OXFAM INTERNATIONAL: working in more than 100 countries to find lasting solutions to poverty, suffering and injustice. **www.oxfam.org**

SWEATSHOP WATCH: committed to eliminating sweatshop conditions in the global garment industry. **www.sweatshopwatch.org**

CONCERN WORLDWIDE: aid group that works with the poor to create just and peaceful societies where the poor can exercise their fundamental rights. **www.concern.net**

ETHICAL TRADING ACTION GROUP: organisers of the No Sweat Campaign. **www.maquilasolidarity.org**

CORPWATCH: a corporate watchdog. **www.corpwatch.org**

RESPONSIBLE SHOPPER: type in a company name and the site will tell you why that company has been both praised and criticised. **www.responsibleshopper.org**

THE CANADIAN CENTRE FOR VICTIMS OF TORTURE: aids survivors to overcome the lasting effects of torture and war, and raises awareness of the continuing effects of torture and war on survivors and their families. **www.ccvt.org**

WORLDWATCH INSTITUTE: working towards an environmentally sustainable society. **www.worldwatch.org**

HUMAN RIGHTS INTERNET: human rights issues. **www.hri.ca**

CORPORATE ACCOUNTABILITY PROJECT: an archive for researching corporations. **www.corporations.org**

CENTER FOR CORPORATE POLICY: a non-partisan public interest organization working to curb corporate abuses and make corporations publicly accountable. **www.corporatepolicy.org**

CITIZEN WORKS: a nonprofit, nonpartisan organization to advance justice by strengthening citizen participation in power. **www.citizenworks.org**

GLOBAL MINING CAMPAIGN: chronicles the human rights, social and environmental abuses that result from modern mining practices. **www.globalminingcampaign.org/theminingnews.html**

MANIFESTO FOR RECEIVING: encourages consumers of culture to increase the longevity of an artist's output by contributing directly to artists rather than utilizing existing economic models. **www.myspace.com/manifestoforreceiving**

Es Konnte auch anders sein.

It could just as well be otherwise.